ow-worms

ages 8–9

elma Page

Egg Poems

Giant Poems

Fox Poems

Sea Poems

Wizard Poems

Space Poems

Introduction

Welcome to *Oxford Reading Tree* Glow-worms Poetry at Stages 8 and 9!

The Glow-worms poetry collections at this stage have been chosen to match topics relevant to the age group. This set includes: eggs, giants, foxes, the sea, wizards and space.

The level of difficulty of the vocabulary broadly matches expectations for Year 3/P4. Although the poetry books are completely independent of *Oxford Reading Tree* stories, it is suggested that they are introduced alongside storybooks at Stages 8 and 9.

This poetry collection

- offers coverage of the NLS requirements for poetry for Year 3/P4 Term 1 in providing poems based on observation and the senses
- develops phonological skills through rhyming words, alliteration and common spelling patterns
- uses a core of high frequency words to help develop children's confidence in reading poetry
- provides illustrations in a range of styles that enhance children's enjoyment of poetry books.

These notes offer support for the teacher by

- listing spelling patterns and rhymes for each poem
- providing notes for a suggested guided/group reading session, based on an objective from the National Literacy Strategy
- suggesting speaking and listening activities, including ways for children to present the poems to an audience
- showing how one of the poems in each collection could be used to develop children's writing
- suggesting independent activities
- opportunities for assessment through observation
- providing a coverage chart to show the teaching objectives coverage for each of the countries in the United Kingdom.

How to introduce the poetry books

You can use these notes to fit your teaching programme, either by selecting an individual poem that supports your literacy objectives or by selecting a book that fits in with your topic work.

- Before reading the poem, introduce the title and talk about the illustrations. Encourage the children to talk about their own experiences and other poems they know.
- Read the poem yourself, at a reasonable pace, so that the children can hear the rhythm and understand the shape and meaning of the whole poem.
- Go back and find memorable words, e.g. "Corn Scratch Kwa Kwa Hen" and "Slink Back Brush Tail Fox".
- Notice imagery and discuss its effectiveness, e.g. "As wide as an oak tree, as tall as a willow".
- Read the poem together, sometimes letting the children predict the rhyming words by themselves.
- Encourage the children to learn a poem so that they can present it to an audience.
- Revisit favourite poems, reading and enjoying them together.

Vocabulary chart

NLS YEAR 3 TERM 1	
EGG POEMS	**Rhymes and spelling patterns**
Egg Hatch	speak/beak watch/hatch cheep/feet
He is Just a Fluffy Chicken	old/gold lot/got
Hatching Eggs	C/me pox/box born/warm squeak/beak free/1B
Wishes	squirm/worm squeal/meal grief/leaf patch/scratch
Cuckoo	nest/best today/lay twigs/eggs ground/sound
Who Can Tell?	tree/me/see steel/real/feel shell/tell
Crack, Chip, Cheep!	wheelbarrow/sparrow watch/hatch straw/saw
Ducks Feeding	bread/fed white/bright feather/together come/crumb
Feeding the Ducks	bread/Ted/instead
The Nest Egg	lay/day any/henny-penny such/much over-loaded/exploded got/lot
GIANT POEMS	**Rhymes and spelling patterns**
Instructions for Giants	pools/schools trees/sneeze layer/chair
Giant Tale	willow/pillow gale/pail tongue/sun Mars/stars
Ogre	belong/long track/back jar/are head/bread
Everything's Giant	ant/pant pea/bee high/by tree/sea
All Giants	all/small me/knee true/too
The Giant Visitor	settee/knee
Fast Food Giant	fries/pies take/shake Mac/Jack
Giant Griff	Griff/cliff sand/stand side/slide

FOX POEMS	Rhymes and spelling patterns
Chicken and Fox	Chicken/ticking time/nine cock/'clock high/fly gun/run tell/well
The Fox and the Crow	three/tree crow/so beak/speak heard/bird below/go tell/well Caw/floor prize/lies
The Rabbit and the Fox	hopping/shopping park/dark stalking/walking tree/me tree/tea bunny/honey me/tea stopping/hopping today/away
The Fox Who Came to Town	clever/over own/down there/fare streets/eat
The Corn Scratch Kwa Kwa Hen and the Fox	grumbling/rumbling Log Dog Scat Cat Brat Rat House Mouse Don't Harm Her Farmer Life Wife Shorter Daughter One Son slip slop/flip flop slick/flick
Foxes Sleeping	bones/home moon/soon take/awake
Red Fox	listening
SEA POEMS	**Rhymes and spelling patterns**
Kites	sway/day/spray grey/away
To the Sea!	row/slow/go/toe/no/snow
Sand	toes/nose bananas/pyjamas hair/everywhere
My Castle	day/away
At the Seaside	
A Week of August Weather	sea/me grey/way through/do sea/tea place/face foam/home sun/fun
The Lighthouse	night/light shone/on plan/fan
The Lightship	bay/away shore/before night/light away/bay
Pebbles	sand/hand old/told lands/bands whales/gales/tales hate/wait beach/teach
The Shell	ear/hear sea/me funfair/there land/sand here/year
Gulls	sand/land cry/sky there/air call/all
WIZARD POEMS	**Rhymes and spelling patterns**
Wizard	box/locks hide/inside shells/spells shoe/to cup/up bird/word spring/sing moon/balloon sill/will
Dear Mr Merlin	day/stay hat/bat long/strong load/toad less/wizardess
Meddling Muddle	boy/Roy stair/there Spell/well fright/right door/floor book/look ten/again cold/told
Ten Things Found in a Wizard's Pocket	
The Wizard Said	south/mouth round/ground cup/up
Just Practising	stood/wood tree/see space/place blizzard/lizard octopus/bus train/again saw/door face/place head/said
Magic Man	suit/flute disappear/ear can/man
SPACE POEMS	**Rhymes and spelling patterns**
Space	Mars/stars U.F.O.'s/toes rays/days guns/suns see/me
The Solar System Tour	thrill/will Mars/stars Moon/soon
Journey Into Space	found/around/crown me/tea
Moonbase Classroom Three	Space/race stars/Mars moon/spoon new/do thrill/brill
Spaceship Race	race/pace whoosh/push behind/mind overtaken/mistaken dinner/winner
The Green Man	night/fright wide/outside small/all plea/tea bread/instead by/fly away/day been/green
Space Message	stars/cars said/dead
From a Space Rocket	Space/face sight/light cease/peace

Curriculum coverage chart

Title	Speaking and listening	Reading	Writing
Egg Poems			
NLS/SLL	Y3T1 28	S2	T14
Scotland	Level B	Level B	Level B
N. Ireland	Activities: a, b Outcomes: b, d, e, f	Activities: a, b, c, e Outcomes: a, b, g	Opportunities: a, b, c Outcomes: a, b, c
Wales	Range: 1, 2, 4 Skills: 1, 2, 5	Range: 3, 5, 6 Skills: 1, 2, 3, 5	Range: 1, 2, 3, 4, 5 Skills: 1, 2, 3, 4
Giant Poems			
NLS/SLL	Y3T1 28	W17	T9
Scotland	Level B	Level B	Level B
N. Ireland	Activities: a, e, f Outcomes: b, c, d, e, f	Activities: a, b, f Outcomes: a, b	Opportunities: a Outcomes: a, b, e
Wales	Range: 1, 2, 4 Skills: 1, 2, 5	Range: 3, 5, 6 Skills: 1, 2, 3, 5	Range: 1, 2, 3, 4, 5 Skills: 1, 2, 3, 4
Fox Poems			
NLS/SLL	Y3T1 26	T3	S9
Scotland	Level B	Level B	Level B
N. Ireland	Activities: a, b, e, f Outcomes: b, d, e, f	Activities: b, c, d Outcomes: a, b, g	Opportunities: a, c Outcomes: a, b, c, e
Wales	Range: 1, 2, 4 Skills: 1, 2, 5	Range: 3, 5, 6 Skills: 1, 2, 3, 5	Range: 1, 2, 3, 4, 5 Skills: 1, 2, 3, 4
Sea Poems			
NLS/SLL	Y3T1 28	T6	T11
Scotland	Level B	Level B	Level B
N. Ireland	Activities: a, b, e, f Outcomes: b, d, e, h	Activities: b, c, f Outcomes: a, b, g	Opportunities a Outcomes: a, b, d, c, f
Wales	Range: 1, 2, 4 Skills: 1, 2, 5	Range: 3, 5, 6 Skills: 1, 2, 3, 5	Range: 1, 2, 3, 4, 5 Skills: 1, 2, 3, 4
Wizard Poems			
NLS/SLL	Y3T1 25	T6	T13
Scotland	Level B	Level B	Level B
N. Ireland	Activities: a, e, f Outcomes: a, c, d	Activities: b, c, e, f Outcomes: a, b, g	Opportunities: a, b, c Outcomes: a, b, c, e
Wales	Range: 1, 2, 4 Skills: 1, 2, 5	Range: 3, 5, 6 Skills: 1, 2, 3, 5	Range: 1, 2, 3, 4, 5 Skills: 1, 2, 3, 4
Space Poems			
NLS/SLL	Y3T1 28	T6	T13
Scotland	Level B	Level B	Level B
N. Ireland	Activities: a, b Outcomes: b, d, e, f	Activities: b, c, e, f Outcomes: a, b, g	Opportunities: a, b, c Outcomes: a, b, c, e
Wales	Range: 1, 2, 4 Skills: 1, 2, 5	Range: 3, 5, 6 Skills: 1, 2, 3, 5	Range: 1, 2, 3, 4, 5 Skills: 1, 2, 3, 4

Egg Poems

Guided/Group reading activities

Objective To take account of the grammar and punctuation, e.g. sentences, speech marks, exclamation marks and commas to mark pauses, when reading aloud (Y3T1 S2).

Cuckoo

- Read the title and then look at the first verse together. Ask the children: *How many sentences are in the first verse?* Check that they notice the commas. Ask one child to read the verse, taking account of the punctuation.
- Ask: *Why do you think the next verse is written in italics?* Ask a child to read the verse. Praise the child for taking the punctuation into account.
- Ask other children to read the next three verses. Focus on the exclamation marks and ask the children to try different ways of reading these sentences to find the right expression.
- Read the whole poem out loud together, using intonation appropriate to the punctuation.

Observing Do the children's readings of the poem take the punctuation into account?

Independent/paired activities

- Ask the children to work with a partner, so that one child is the narrator and the other is the cuckoo. Ask them to decide which parts of the poem each should read. Encourage them to practise reading with expression that matches the punctuation and to then perform the poem to the group or class.
- Ask the children to read "The Nest Egg" (page 16) to themselves. Ask them to look closely at the punctuation. Let them practise reading the poem aloud before performing it to the group or class.

Speaking and listening activities

Objective To present events and characters through dialogue to engage the interest of an audience (Y3T1 28).

Wishes

- Ask the children to find the author of this poem. Tell the children that "Anon" is short for "Anonymous" and that we do not know the author's name.
- Read the poem together, and then ask: *How many characters are in this poem?*
- Ask three children to say the words of the three chicks and ask one to be the mother.
- Ask a fifth child to be the narrator. Point out that each verse is read partly by the narrator and partly by a chick or the mother.
- Ask the children to practise reading the poem so that there are no gaps between when the narrator and chicks are speaking.
- Praise the children for being aware when it is their turn to read. Encourage the chicks to read their parts with expression.
- Ask the children to read the poem out loud to the class.

Observing Check that the children:

- try different voices for the chicks
- engage the interest of the audience.

Writing

Objective To invent calligrams and a range of shape poems, selecting appropriate words and careful presentation. Build up class collections (Y3T1 T14).

Ducks Feeding

- Read the poem together. Look for all the adjectives and make a list, e.g. "rare", "common", "coloured".
- Use the picture to add more colours and descriptions to the list. Add the body part, e.g. "green head", "white neck" "brown breast", "blue flash", "yellow beak."
- Make up a list poem together, naming the colour of each body part.
- Present the poem as a calligram, using colours to write the colour words. You could do this on the computer or using coloured pencils.
- You could also make this a shape poem by writing in the outline of a duck, making the lines fit the duck shape.
- Ask the children to write their own calligrams about other birds.

Observing Are the children able to suggest lines for the poem? Do they understand that they can make the calligraphy of the poem reflect the meaning of the words?

Giant Poems

Guided/Group reading activities

Objective To generate synonyms for high frequency words (Y3T1 W17).

The Giant Visitor

- Read poem together.
- Ask the children to find "great big" each time it appears in the poem.
- Make a list of the phrases, e.g. "great big foot", "great big stocking".
- Ask the children to think of an alternative adjective for "great big" in each phrase, e.g. "Enormous foot", "gigantic stocking".
- Try to adjust your new adjectives so that they fit the rhythm of the poem.
- Read the poem, substituting the synonyms.
- Read the original poem again and decide which version you like best.

Observing Are the children able to suggest synonyms for "great big"?

Independent/paired activities

- Tell the children to change the poem's title to "The Tiny Visitor". Ask them to think of words that describe very small things, and to then say or write the poem, substituting their "small" words for "great big" each time it appears.
- Ask the children to read "All Giants" on page 11. Ask them to make a list of words that can be used instead of "said", e.g. "announced" in the first line. Ask the children to write or say the poem, putting in synonyms instead of "said". Discuss which words sound better than "said".

Speaking and listening activities

Objective To present events and characters through dialogue to engage the interest of an audience (Y3T1 28).

Fast Food Giant

- Ask the children: *What is "Fast Food"? What kinds of food do you get in a fast food restaurant?*
- Read the poem together. Ask: *Who is the narrator? Is it the boy or the giant? How can you tell?*
- Talk about the way the poem is written as an order in a fast food restaurant.
- Ask: *Can you think of anything else he might have ordered?*
- Ask: *What does Jack imagine the giant saying? Why does Jack think the giant will say, "When's lunch Jack?"?*
- Ask the children to suggest ways to read the poem. Praise them for showing in their reading when Jack is ordering food, and when he is speaking in the giant's voice.
- Ask the children to practise before reading the poem aloud to the group or class.

Observing Check that the children:

- are able to use appropriate voices for the characters
- engage the attention of the audience when they read the poem aloud.

Writing

Objective To generate ideas relevant to a topic by brainstorming, word association, etc. (Y3T1 T9).

Instructions for Giants

- Ask the children to imagine that a giant is visiting the school. Ask: *What could a giant tread on or sit on and spoil without noticing?*
- Ask the children to think of any ideas that come to mind. Make a list of the things the giant should look out for.
- Ask: *What could a giant do to be helpful?* Together, make a list of things that the giant would be able to do.
- Read the poem. Add to your list of things the giant must be careful not to do.
- Add more things that the giant can do to help.
- Ask the children to think of possible titles for two posters, one telling the giant to be careful, and the other asking the giant to help.
- Make a list of the ideas for titles.
- Ask the children to use the brainstorm lists to write posters, either telling the giant to be careful, or asking him for help.

Observing Can the children add ideas to the lists? Can they suggest possible titles?

Fox Poems

Guided/Group reading activities

Objective To be aware of the different voices in stories using dramatised readings, showing differences between the narrator and different characters used, e.g. puppets to present stories (Y3T1 T3).

The Rabbit and the Fox

- Read the poem through together.
- Look at the lines with speech marks and ask the children to decide whether the rabbit or the fox is speaking.
- Ask one of the children to be the rabbit, and another to be the fox. Encourage them to experiment with voices by reading just the lines that the animals say.
- Re-read the lines that a narrator would read. Point out the repetition and ask the children to try out ways to read these lines. Decide what sounds effective.
- Ask three children to be the three voices of the poem (the fox, the rabbit and the narrator). Praise them for reading with distinctive voices.
- The children could use rabbit and fox masks or puppets to present the poem to the rest of the class or the school.

Observing Are the children able to identify three distinct voices in the poem? Can they read the poem in a dramatised form?

Independent/paired activities

- Ask the children to work with a partner and make up a conversation between a rabbit and a fox. The fox tries to tempt the rabbit and the rabbit makes up reasons not to go with him.
- Ask the children to practise reading "The Fox and the Crow" on page 4. Ask them to find where a narrator and where a character speaks. Encourage the children to use different voices for the characters and the narrator. Let them practise reading the poem before reading it to the group.

Speaking and listening activities

Objective To follow up others' points and show whether they agree or disagree in a whole-class discussion (Y3T1 26).

The Corn Scratch Kwa Kwa Hen and the Fox

- Read the title and talk about the name of the hen. Ask: *How do you think the poet thought of this name?*
- Read the poem together. Ask: *Why are some words in bold capital letters?*
- Talk about what happens in the story.
- Ask: *What do you notice about the rhymes in this poem?* Look for the rhymes and make a list, e.g. "grumbling rumbling".
- Ask: *Did you notice words that sound like their meaning?* Find all the words, such as "slip slop", "flip flop", "scatter", "clatter".
- Talk about ways to read the poem, varying the speed of reading and the volume of sound.
- Think of actions that represent the descriptions and events in the poem, e.g. cupping their hands when the hen whispers.
- Re-read the poem using the presentation you have chosen.
- Present the poem to the class or to the rest of the school.

Observing Check that the children:

- comment on the poem
- say whether they agree or disagree with other children's comments.

Writing

Objective To notice and investigate a range of other devices for presenting texts, e.g. speech bubbles, enlarged or italicised print, captions and headings, inset text. Explore purpose and collect examples (Y3T1 S9).

The Fox and the Crow

- Look at the presentation of the poem with the children and ask: *What do you notice about the pictures for this poem?* Check that they notice there is a picture for each verse, and that it is a bit like a comic strip.
- Read the poem together.
- Suggest changing the presentation into a series of pictures with speech and thought bubbles.
- Re-read the first verse. Draw a thought bubble on a piece of paper, and ask: *How can we tell this part of the poem by saying what the crow is thinking?* Cut out the thought bubble and fix it onto the page beside the picture with reusable adhesive.
- Read the next verse, and ask: *What shall we write in the fox's speech bubble?*
- Continue with the poem, writing what the fox says and what the crow thinks.
- Re-read all the thought and speech bubbles. Decide whether they retell the main points of the story, or if something has been left out. Make changes if you need to.
- Re-read the poem and ask the children whether they like their version or the original poem best. Ask for their reasons.

Observing Are the children able to use speech and thought bubbles to rewrite the story of the poem? Can they say whether the new presentation retold the story effectively?

Sea Poems

Guided/Group reading activities

Objective To read aloud and recite poems, comparing different views of the same subject; to discuss choice of words and phrases that describe and create impact, e.g. adjectives, powerful and expressive verbs (Y3T1 T6).

Pebbles/The Shell

- Read the title, "Pebbles", and ask: *How is a pebble different from a stone?* You could use a dictionary to check the definitions.
- Read "Pebbles" together. Ask the children to find the words that describe the pebble.
- Read the poem again, and ask: *Which words paint vivid pictures in our minds?* Find "fierce bands", "mighty fighting fish" and other words and phrases that the children suggest.
- Read "The Shell" together, and ask: *What is different about this poem?*
- Discuss the quieter sounds in the poem and ask the children to find the words that achieve this, e.g. "ear", "hear", "sea", "me", "wading", "whispering". Point out how the softer consonants (e.g. "w", "h", "sh", and "th") achieve a sleepy sound.
- Ask: *Which poem did you like best? Which poem reminds you most of the sea?*

Observing Are the children able to identify words and phrases that have impact in the two poems? Can they compare the two poems?

Independent/paired activities

- Ask the children to read "The Lighthouse" and "The Lightship" on pages 12–13. Ask them to think of one way in which the poems are similar, and one way in which they are different. Ask the children to explain their ideas to the group.
- Ask the children to read "Kites" on page 2. Ask them to make a list of the "–ing" words in the poem. Ask them to think of some more "–ing" words that describe a kite, e.g. climbing, soaring.

Speaking and listening activities

Objective To present events and characters through dialogue to engage the interest of an audience (Y3T1 28).

Sand

- Talk about sand on the seashore with the children. Ask: *What do you like about sand? What do you dislike about it?*
- Read the poem together. Tell the group that you would like them to perform this poem for younger listeners. Ask: *How can we act out this poem as we say it?*
- Read the poem line by line and discuss actions that might fit. Try out different suggestions and ask the children to say which they think are more effective.
- When you have suggestions for a verse, go back and say that verse, doing the actions. Ask the children to say whether they think the effect is good enough. Ask: *How can we make it even better?*
- Ask: *Does the poem sound fun? How can we make sure that younger children will enjoy it?*
- Experiment with different expression and emphasis, e.g. on the words "bananas" and "pyjamas".
- Let the children practise and then perform the poem to a younger audience.

Observing Check that the children:

- are able to think of ways to make this poem interesting to a younger audience
- retain the interest of their audience while performing the poem.

Writing

Objective To develop the use of settings in own stories by writing short descriptions of known places; writing a description in the style of a familiar story (Y3T1 T11).

Gulls

- Read "Gulls" together. Find words and phrases in the poem that show the setting, e.g. "sea shore", "sand", "face to the water", "back to the land".
- Re-read the poem, and then ask: *What do you remember about this poem?* Talk about the sounds of the gulls and the loneliness of the boy.
- Ask the children to think of other words and phrases that describe a seashore setting. Make a list of sounds, sights and smells.
- Ask the children to imagine they are the child in the picture. Ask them to write a description of what they can see, hear and smell as they stand on the seashore.
- Let the children read the descriptions to each other. Talk about the words and phrases that best create an image of the seashore.

Observing Are the children able to think of their own ways of describing the seashore? Can they identify strong images in their own and each other's work?

Wizard Poems

Guided/Group reading activities

Objective To read aloud and recite poems, comparing different views of the same subject; to discuss choice of words and phrases that describe and create impact, e.g. adjectives, powerful and expressive verbs (Y3T1 T6).

Wizard/Just Practising

- Read the poem, "Wizard", together.
- Find and talk about all the magic things the wizard is going to do. Ask: *Which thing do you think is the most impressive?*
- Ask: *Which lines do you like best? What do you like about them?*
- Read the lines about the moon. Ask: *How does the poet describe the moon? How does it help you build a picture in your mind?*
- Read the poem, "Just Practising".
- Talk about the spells the wizard creates. Re-read the poem, and then ask: *Which lines to you like most?* Discuss effective phrases, such as "crouched with thumping hearts" and "a waiting stillness".
- Ask: *Which of the poems did you enjoy most? Can you say why?*

Observing Are the children able to pick out the words and phrases that held their attention? Can they say which lines they liked best and why? Can they compare the two poems?

Independent/paired activities

- Ask the children to choose one of these two poems ("Wizard" or "Just Practising") and practise reading it aloud. Let them present it to the group.
- Ask the children to choose any other poem in the book. Ask them to practise reading it so that they can read it to the group. Ask them to say which lines they like best and why.

Speaking and listening activities

Objective To explain a process or present information, ensuring items are clearly sequenced, relevant details included and accounts ended effectively (Y3T1 25).

Meddling Muddle

- Read the poem together or independently.
- Ask the children to close their books, and then retell the poem as a story. Ask one member of the group to begin, then another to say what happened next.
- If anyone disagrees, or thinks something has been left out, they must put up their hand, and not interrupt the speaker.
- Give the children time to explain and justify their ideas. Discuss any dissenting ideas, and then turn to the book to see who is right.
- You may need to re-state the main points of the story from time to time to keep track of events.
- Praise children for making their points sensibly, and for backing up their ideas with the text.

Observing

Check that the children:

- co-operate to retell the story
- recall the correct sequence of events and include relevant detail.

Writing

Objective To collect suitable words and phrases, in order to write poems and short descriptions; design simple patterns with words, use repetitive phrases; write imaginative comparisons (Y3T1 T13).

Ten Things Found in a Wizard's Pocket

- Read the poem and look at the way the words and illustrations are combined on the page.
- Ask the children to find the shortest item and the longest item. Focus on how the descriptions make the list more interesting than a list of ten words.
- Look more carefully at each item to find out what makes it special. Ask: *Is it unusual or impossible?*
- Ask the children to think of some more strange things that a witch or wizard might keep in a pocket.
- Ask the children to make up their own list. Remind them to make each item special.
- Use the same layout as the poem's to write and illustrate the ten new items. The poems could be used in a display.
- Ask the children to take turns to read their lists to the group. Ask the children to say which item in each other's list they like best and why.

Observing Are the children able to think of more unusual items? Do they show that they understand the need to make the items surprising? Do they use interesting words to describe them?

Space Poems

Guided/Group reading activities

Objective To read aloud and recite poems, comparing different views of the same subject; to discuss choice of words and phrases that describe and create impact, e.g. adjectives, powerful and expressive verbs (Y3T1 T6).

Space Message/From a Space Rocket

- Read the poem, "Space Message", together. Ask the children: *What was the message from space?*
- Look for words and phrases that make the spaceman sound alien, such as "distant kingdom" and "garment of silver".
- Read the poem, "From a Space Rocket". Ask: *What is the message of this poem?* Talk about the idea that, if viewed from space, all our worries seem trivial.
- Ask: *Which verses and lines do you think are memorable?*
- Talk about the way the poet has chosen words that illustrate his idea of the Earth from space, e.g. "mountains and oceans were turned to pure light."
- Ask: *Which poem do you think was more effective?* Encourage the children to refer to words from the poem as they give their reasons.

Observing Are the children able to compare the two poems? Can they identify effective words and phrases in the poems?

Independent/paired activities

- Ask the children to work with a partner and read "From a Space Rocket" again. Ask them to make a list of words and phrases that they like in the poem, such as "rolling through Space". Encourage them to think of some more words that they can use to write about space, such as "planets" and "asteroids". Ask the children to add an adjective to each noun (e.g. "unknown planets", "rocky asteroids").
- Ask the children to draw the spaceman with a speech bubble. Ask them to write a message from the spaceman to the people on Earth in the speech bubble.

Speaking and listening activities

Objective To present events and characters through dialogue to engage the interest of an audience (Y3T1 28).

The Solar System Tour

- Read the title and the first verse, and then ask the children to look at the picture. Ask the children: *What is the speaker trying to do?*
- Talk about places where people try to interest us in a ride, or encourage us to buy something, e.g. a funfair, a market.
- Read the rest of the poem. Ask: *Does the speaker make you want to have a ride? Which lines made you feel you wanted to go?*
- Try out ways of reading the poem aloud. Ask: *How can we make people interested in coming on the tour?*
- Ask: *Why is "know" in italics? Can we read the word in a way that emphasises it?"*
- Ask the children to find all the lines that end in exclamation marks. Ask different children to read single lines, showing by their expression that there is an exclamation mark at the end.
- Ask children to say what they like about the way other children read.
- Let children practise reading the whole poem before presenting it to the class.

Observing Check that the children:

- are able to present the poem in a persuasive manner
- engage the attention of the audience.

Writing

Objective To collect suitable words and phrases, in order to write poems and short descriptions; design simple patterns with words, use repetitive phrases; write imaginative comparisons (Y3T1 T13).

Journey Into Space

- Read the poem, emphasising the repetition. Ask: *Why do you think the poet has repeated these phrases?*
- Change the name "Jaswinder" to a child's name from the group. Ask: *Does the new name fit the rhythm of the poem?*
- Try out different names and decide which one sounds best.
- Ask the children to identify other words that they could change, e.g. "sunrise" instead of "daybreak", "Martians" instead of "aliens".
- Read the poem again, making the changes the children have decided upon.
- Ask the children to write a "Journey Into Space" poem. Encourage them to use the structure of the original poem, but change as many words as they can.
- Read the new poems to the group.

Observing Are the children able to use repetitive phrases in their own work?

Links to other Oxford Reading Tree titles

- Jackdaws Anthologies at Stages 8 and 9
- Magpies Stories at Stages 8 and 9
- Magpies Playscripts at Stage 8
- Treetops All Stars
- Web Poetry
- Web Fiction

OXFORD
UNIVERSITY PRESS

Great Clarendon Street, Oxford OX2 6DP

Oxford University Press is a department of the University of Oxford. It furthers the University's objective of excellence in research, scholarship, and education by publishing worldwide in

Oxford New York

Auckland Cape Town Dar es Salaam Hong Kong Karachi Kuala Lumpur Madrid Melbourne Mexico City Nairobi New Delhi Shanghai Taiper Toronto

With offices in

Argentina Austria Brazil Chile Czech Republic France Greece Guatemala Hungary Italy Japan Poland Portugal Singapore South Korea Switzerland Thailand Turkey Ukraine Vietnam

First published 2004

British Library Cataloguing in Publication Data

Data available

Cover illustrations by Lindy Norton

Teacher's Notes: ISBN 978-0-19-845490-8

10 9

Page make-up by IFA Design Ltd, Plymouth, Devon

Printed in China by Imago